Mt Rainier Awakening

On the Verge of Eruption and Devastating Destruction

A prophetic warning!

Scientists are predicting Mt Rainier will erupt at any time but when—they cannot tell. However, God knows exactly when this last day's event will occur and He warns his servants beforehand to prepare.

Charles Pretlow

Mt Rainier Awakening
On the Verge of Eruption and Devastating Destruction
August 3, 2025

Mt Rainier Awakening (July 2025) (Includes "God is Raising His Voice")
ISBN 978-1-943412-22-8

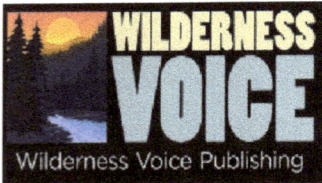

Published by
Wilderness Voice Publishing
PO Box 857
Canon City, CO 81215

"A voice crying in the wilderness –
proclaiming the good news of the coming Kingdom!"

Prophecy Timeline

- First prophesy received, March 29, 2012
- First put in print April 2012
- Second prophesy received May 2014
- First Message Published August 2014
  Includes "God is Raising His Voice")
- Update Published June 2018
- 2nd Edition Published August 2025

Rainier Awakening

On the Verge of Eruption and Devastating Destruction

Contents

Introduction

"And in the last days it shall be, God declares, that I will pour out my Spirit on all flesh, and your sons and your daughters shall prophesy, and your young men shall see visions, and your old men shall dream dreams; even on my male servants and female servants in those days I will pour out my Spirit, and they shall prophesy" (Acts 2:17-18).

Every sincere student of Christ's words should be realizing that we are living in the last moments of this age.

All the signs Christ said to watch for are coming together in this generation—they are playing-out right before our eyes. Yet most Christians are numb to these warnings as they enjoy the pleasures of life that the world offers.

The above passage from the book of Acts describes how the Holy Spirit will use the Lord's servants to prophesy (forewarn) as to what is coming upon the world, the masses of people, and Christ's church. This includes prophesy, visions and dreams.

Dreams have been given to me starting back in 1974. These dreams come in such a manner that leaves no doubt they are of God. In the beginning most dreams were given for personal direction, later warning dreams about trouble coming upon the world, especially America were given.

In March 2012 a dream was given to me about the Pacific Northwest (Puget Sound area), where lava, ash, and forest fires consumed much of the area.

I shared this warning with others in our fellowship, and we prayed for more time before any catastrophic event took place—so that Christians in this region would awaken and become ready.

Then in 2014 the Lord gave a more specific warning dream. In this dream the west slope of Mt. Rainier blew up spewing lava and ash.

We did nothing about this dream and sought the Lord for direction. Then in 2018 when the volcano in Hawaii erupted, we felt it was time to publish the dream about Mt Rainier. **That first publication is included in this update.**

From 2014 until now, Mt Rainier has mostly been silent with normal background tremors and gas releases. However, in April and May of this year (2025) all the signs of an imminent eruption began occurring.

So serious were these swarms of earthquakes and other signs of potential eruption, with abnormal gas releases a Red Alert was sounded and transmitted. Then another recent swarm of earthquake hit Mt Rainier on July 10th with more than 400 taking place.

It was in late April 2025, that the USGS (United States Geological Survey) monitoring Mt Rainier sounded a red alert [1] warning, while detecting swarms of earthquakes (not tremors) were occurring in large amounts (in one week over 500,) with more than normal gas release. In addition, USCG through satellite imagery, that measures the manga underneath the mountain was enlarging.

Not many responded to the red alert and most likely for fear of causing panic, the red alert was cancelled.

Then on July 8th another swarm of small earthquakes was detected early in the morning by the U.S. Geological Survey and the University of Washington. <u>No Red Alert was given!</u>

The Pacific Northwest is sitting a ticking time bomb, and thousands upon thousands are unprepared.

In the 1st edition (included in this publication) it includes help for the reader to gain an understanding of deadly threat ready to entomb hundreds in the massive flow of hot lava, mud, water, and structural debris.

You will read in this edition (the 2nd edition) more specific information on what to expect and why God is allowing this judgment to take place.

---

[1] **Red Alert:** Satellites caught the mountain swelling and within hours the USGS raised a red alert. Now scientists warn this could ignite a West Coast catastrophe.

Red Alert

Swarms of Earthquakes Under Mt Rainier

One of the major signs that scientists insist on being acutely aware of are swarms of shallow earthquakes underneath an active volcano. Suddenly, Mt Rainier is experiencing swarms of shallow earthquakes. This started in April and May and occurred again in July and continues at sporadic times. Mt. Rainier is not the only volcano with an increase in volcanic, earthquakes and volcanic activity—all around the Pacific Ocean volcanic activity is taking place.

Pacific Rim of Fire

8   Mt Rainier Awaking

The following news headlines should be alarming:

"Monitoring stations detect small magnitude earthquakes at Mount Rainier during July 2025" (USCG).

"Larger swarm than anything we've seen': Rainier quakes reach historic levels" (Tacoma News Review).

"Officials are tracking an earthquake swarm at Mount Rainier but say there is no cause for concern" (America Online).

Mt Rainier is part of the Pacific Rim of Fire (volcanos) and is awakening again. In reviewing the above map, you can see how the whole Pacific Ocean is ringed with active and dormant volcanoes. As I am writing this section, an 8.8 magnitude earthquake struck just off the western coast of Russia. Read Fox News headline: "Monster Quake, One of the largest earthquakes ever recorded strikes off coast of Russia."

Rainier has had minor activities with the last full eruption occurring some 1,000 years ago. This eruption produced a large lahar [2] (major mud flow system). Scientists say that Mt Rainier is ready to have a major eruption at any time—but when is impossible to tell.

Major mud flows are a giant topic of concern. From the eruption of Mt St. Helens in 1980 the local communities experienced massive destruction down the Tootle river, and other tributaries, loss of homes, deaths and the

One of the home lost on the Toutle River

I-5 Bridge over the Toutle River

---

[2] A lahar: is a violent type of mudflow or debris flow composed of a slurry of pyroclastic material, rocky debris and water. The material flows down from a volcano, typically along a river valley. Lahars are often extremely destructive and deadly; they can flow tens of meters per second, they have been known to be up to 140 meters (460 ft) deep, and large flows tend to destroy any structures in their path.

weakening superstructures, such as weakening of bridges on I-5. The river water was steaming hot and cooked wildlife and humans caught in its path. Homes were cemented in with the Lara debris, others crushed and washed down river.

Why Mount Rainier is the US volcano that troubles scientists most By Katie Hunt, CNN June 26, 2024

"Mount Rainier keeps me up at night because it poses such a great threat to the surrounding communities. Tacoma and South Seattle are built on 100-foot-thick (30.5-meter) ancient mudflows from eruptions of Mount Rainier," Jess Phoenix, a volcanologist and ambassador for the Union of Concerned Scientists, said on an episode of **"Violent Earth With Liv Schreiber,"** a CNN Original Series.

The sleeping giant's destructive potential lies not with fiery flows of lava, which, in the event of an eruption, would be unlikely to extend more than a few miles beyond the boundary of Mount Rainier National Park in the Pacific Northwest. And the majority of volcanic ash would likely dissipate downwind to the east away from population centers, according to the US Geological Survey.

"The thing that makes Mount Rainier tough is that it is so tall, and it's covered with ice and snow, and so if there is any kind of eruptive activity, hot stuff … will melt the cold stuff and a lot of water will start coming down," said Seth Moran, a research seismologist at USGS Cascades Volcano Observatory in Vancouver, Washington.

"And there are tens, if not hundreds of thousands of people who live in areas that potentially could be impacted by a large lahar, and it could happen quite quickly."

The deadliest Lahar in recent memory was in November 1985 when Colombia's Nevado del Ruiz volcano erupted. Just a couple hours after the eruption started, a river of mud, rocks, lava and icy water swept over the town of Armero, killing over 23,000 people in a matter of minutes.

"When it comes to rest … you've got this hardened almost, like, concrete substance that can be like quicksand when people are trying to get out of it," said Bradley Pitcher, a volcanologist and lecturer in Earth and environmental sciences at Columbia University, said in an episode of CNN's **"Violent Earth."**

Pitcher said that Mount Rainier has about eight times the number of glaciers and snow as Nevado del Ruiz had when it erupted. **"There's the potential to have a much more catastrophic mudflow."**

Building Towards a Catastrophic Eruption

What the Lord showed us about Mt Rainier's Forthcoming Eruption

Scientists know Mount Rainier is due to experiencing a catastrophic eruption at any time but have no way of exactly knowing when this will occur.

The following news headlines should awaken individuals to relocate now, if possible, especially those living in the old Lahar zones or close to Mt Rainier:

> `"Larger swarm than anything we've seen':` `Rainier quakes reach historic levels."` Tacoma News Tribune 7/16/2025

> `"Is Mt. Rainier About To Blow? Earthquake Swarm At Volcano Continues."` News Radio 560 KPQ 7/15/2025

> `Volcanoes are turning in their sleep across the US. What does that mean for Washington? A recent earthquake swarm at Mount Rainier in Washington state, along with increased volcanic activity in Alaska, Oregon, and Hawaii."` Kitsap Sun 7/15/2025

> `"Officials are tracking an earthquake swarm at Mount Rainier but say there is no cause for concern— Officials are tracking the largest swarm of earthquakes in more than 15 years on Washington's Mount Rainier but say there is no cause for alarm."` SEATTLE (AP) 7/15/2025

In April 2025 seven major indicators of a potential eruption were detected by USGS causing a red alert.

1. Mt. Rainier has over 18 glaciers that are melting.
2. Swarms of small quakes underneath the mountain are beginning to occur.
3. Heat from the quakes is melting glaciers.
4. Unusual Gas Releases.
5. A strange pulse occurs exactly every 11 minutes.
6. Satellite indicates that the lava dome is increasing in size.
7. Satellite detected a lava tunnel connecting Mt Rainier to Mt Saint Hellens and continuing on to Mt Hood in Oregon.

Why did the USGS end the red alert so quickly? Scientists sound red alert when they are sure they know an eruption is in process. All the above listed precursors and abnormalities happening certainly seemed like an eruption was starting.

Then when the eruption did not take place in minutes, the red alert was called off.

A sustained red alert would have caused panic, chaos, accidents, death and great financial loss. The way Mt Rainier is acting is causing scientific analysis to become guess work.

The "For Sure Thing" is to Hear Rightly From God

No one on Earth knows the precise time MT Rainier will erupt, yet every sincere and dedicated Christian can be disciplined to hear the true voice of God and learn to obey.

There are many accounts in Scripture where servants of God and followers of Christ were forewarned by the Holy Spirit or an Angel to get out of the way of disaster.

God will use his prophets and servants to forewarn. The most renown prophet is the Lord Jesus Christ himself. It is Jesus who laid out the signs to watch for concerning his return and end of this age troubles and judgments.

Concerning earthquakes and volcanos, Christ warned that in the last days different things would announce his soon return. Here is what he said about earthquakes: *"For nation will rise against nation, and kingdom against kingdom, and there will be famines and earthquakes in various places"* (Matthew 24:7).

Just today (8/3/25) I read Fox News headline: **"Massive volcano blasts ash miles into sky, marking first eruption in 475 years."** Two days prior to this eruption, in the same area of Russia, an 8.8 magnitude earthquake shook the whole area are causing tsunami warnings.

What the Lord showed us about Mt Rainier's Eruption: The 2014 dream showed Mt Rainier's west slope erupting, spewing molten lava for miles. In the dream the weather was clear and warm, like a hot summer's day. With all the activity under and around Mt Rainier and around the Pacific Rim of Fire, after team prayer we sensed that in within a couple of years, during summer months, June, July, August and September, Mt. Rainier will most likely erupt causing much loss of life and property damage. God is giving time for people living in this region of the Pacific Northwest to be prepared and even relocate.

If Possible, Relocate Now: If you rent it may be easier to relocate. Selling property will be challenging. You must seek the Lord on what to do. The number one thing to take into consideration is if you live in an old Lahar valley. Those old mud flow valleys will act like funnels filling up with mud, water, debris homes, vehicles, dead animals and dead people.

A Minute's Notice to Evacuate: If you must stay, be prepared to leave in a matter of minutes. This means that you must have your survival equipment packed and ready to be put in your vehicle. Make a check list. Get to highest ground immediately. Stay out of the way National Guard, Firefighters, and Law enforcement.

Store Up Food, Water, Fuel, and other basic survival items: Do this now, if you wait your local store will be emptied.

Good Temporary Lodging, Tents, Travel Trailer if Possible: In advance, establish a safe place to go to. Procure enough camping resources, food, and water to last 60 days. Make sure you have written permission if it is private property. The roads, especially in the Lahar areas, will be jammed with frantic drivers. Plan your escape route to avoid terrified drivers.

Stay Away from the Crowds (Criminals/Looters): We live in the last days, where Jesus said lawlessness would abound, and learn how to discern and avoid evil people.

Become Aware of Self-Defense Options and Enroll in Classes.

Again—Stay Away from the Lahars: Get to the Highest Ground Possible.

Obtain Permission in advance to Setup Temporary Living Quarters. Make sure you have Trustworthy Transportation.

Stay in Continuous Connection with the Authorities: Radio, shortwave handsets. Do not listen to the rumor mill, unless you know the person and verify.

These are just a few commonsense suggestions. Good survival books are available at just about any sports store, or online through a dependable retail store such as Amazon.

-3-
Signs of the Close of this Age
Stay Awake and be Prepared

Over the last 75 years most Christians have been taught that at the end of this age there would be no suffering—the clouds will disappear, and the sky will open up like scroll. This is how the rapture will begin, as Jesus sends out his angels to collect true Christians worldwide just before the Great Tribulation begins with the revealing of the antichrist. This false doctrine allows Christians to take their ease. <u>This is not what Jesus taught, read Christ's words on the rapture:</u>

"And if the Lord had not cut short the days, no human being would be saved. But for the sake of the elect, whom he chose, he shortened the days" (Mark 13:20).
   <u>(The Lord will shorten those days, when the antichrist comes to rule and the great tribulation starts).</u>

"But in those days, after that tribulation, the sun will be darkened, and the moon will not give its light, and the stars will be falling from heaven, and the powers in the heavens will be shaken. And then they will see the Son of Man coming in clouds with great power and glory. And then he will send out the angels and gather his elect from the four winds, from the ends of the earth to the ends of heaven" (Mark 13:24-27).
   <u>(These remarks by our Lord clearly indicate that the number of days that the Great Tribulation will cause much suffering and pain, will be cut short for the sake of the Christian. The gathering of the elect is what is called the rapture—the removal of true and faithful believers from the Earth).</u>

Read what the Apostle Paul wrote about the rapture: *"For the Lord himself will descend from heaven with a cry of command, with the voice of an archangel, and with the sound of the trumpet of God. And the dead in Christ will rise first. Then we who are alive, who are left, will be caught up together with them in the clouds to meet the Lord in the air, and so we will always be with the Lord. Therefore encourage one another with these words"* (1 Thessalonians 4:16-18).

Jesus said to pay attention to the signs of his coming:
(Just as the scientist are paying close attention to signs that Mt Rainier is ready to erupt, so should every child of God know and recognize the signs of Christ's coming).

"And there will be signs in sun and moon and stars, and on the earth distress of nations in perplexity because of the roaring of the sea and the waves, people fainting with fear and with foreboding of what is coming on the world. For the powers of the heavens will be shaken. And then they will see the Son of Man coming in a cloud with power and great glory. Now when these things begin to take place, straighten up and raise your heads, because your redemption is drawing near" (Luke 21:25-28).

Jesus said to stay awake and not become bogged down: *"But watch yourselves lest your hearts be weighed down with dissipation and drunkenness and cares of this life, and that day come upon you suddenly like a trap. For it will come upon all who dwell on the face of the whole earth. But stay awake at all times, praying that you may have strength to escape all these things that are going to take place, and to stand before the Son of Man"* (Luke 21:34-36).

Jesus said we would not know the day or hour of his coming: However, we will know the season, and thus we must be prepared. Just as scientists do not know when Mt Rainier will erupt, they can judge the closeness of the event based on the signs that lead to an eruption.

When these things begin to take place: Jesus gave a description of all the abnormalities that will take place that indicate Christ's soon return. Do you know these things? Study Scripture yourself, don't take someone elses word, interpretations, and opinions.

If you carefully study Christ words and the New Testament, you will see that these things are taking place right now. One of the most obvious is the cultures in the world, especially America turning vile, lawless, and carefree. Jesus said that the last days would be like the days of Noah and Sodom.

When there is peace and security: In the American culture, it is very easy to see how perversion and happy-go-lucky mentality yet living under the threat of war and economic troubles has become. The Apostle Paul wrote of this time that we are in now: *"For you yourselves are fully aware that the day of the Lord will come like a thief in the night. While people are saying, 'There is peace and security,' then sudden destruction will come upon them as* *labor pains come upon a pregnant woman, and they will not escape"* (1 Thessalonians 5:2-3).

America groaned for peace, security, and prosperity under the Biden administration. Now that Trump is President is in office just about everything is looking good and being called America's golden age.

The American mindset is drawing dangerously close in matching the Apostle Paul's warning; *"While people are saying, 'There is peace and security,' then sudden destruction will come upon them."*

Like those who live close to Mt Rainier, we must all be prepared to survive the many disasters and lawlessness increasing worldwide.

Jesus warned: *"But stay awake at all times, praying that you may have strength to escape all these things that are going to take place, and to stand before the Son of Man"* (Luke 21:36).

The Apostle John's vision of the end time (in the book of Revelation) has a haunting passage about Christians in the last days who live in a Babylonian-like empire that looks very much like the American society.

"Then I heard another voice from heaven saying, "Come out of her, my people, lest you take part in her sins, lest you share in her plagues" (Revelation 18:4).

Most Americans are enthralled with America, her economic prowess, and Trump's vision for the future, which he has called "America's Golden Age." America is morphing into Revelation's Babylon, it is time for Christians to have their hearts set things that are above, walking in the fulness of Christ.

Give Up the Love for America and things of this world, for the kingdom of Heaven is at our doorsteps, ready for Christ to appear, return, and set up the Kingdom of heaven on Earth.

Read the First Edition published in 2014

God is Raising Hi Voice 1ˢᵗ Edition August 2014

ISBN 978-0-98012768-6-5

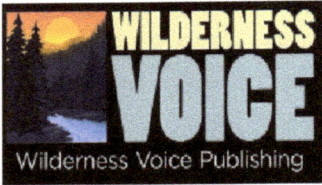

Published by
Wilderness Voice Publishing
PO Box 857
Canon City, CO 81215

"A voice crying in the wilderness –
proclaiming the good news of the coming Kingdom!"

Contents

About this Prophetic Message

Wilderness Voice Publishing is dedicated to bringing forth timely messages and prophetic warnings to help the sincere Christian wake up before the midnight cry awakening. (Matthew 25:1-13 last days parable of the ten virgins.)

This prophecy was first printed in April 2012 but was not released publicly. It was published in August 2014 for distribution to the public.

Though this warning was published in 2014, we did nothing to promote this prophetic message. With the May 2018 volcanic activity starting up on the Big Island of Hawaii, the Lord prompted me to send this message to those who will be most affected by MT Rainier's eruption.

We are not sure when this prophecy will come to pass. Jesus prophesied that the 2nd Temple would be destroyed and implied it would be soon, and the Pharisees and other temple leaders mocked him. That prophecy finally came to pass forty years after it was given.

Introduction

Originally from the Pacific Northwest, my heart is burdened with what the Lord has shown me coming to the Puget Sound area.

This warning is meant for the sincere Christian who knows Christ, who has an ear to hear what the Spirit is saying to God's people in this hour—and particularly to the churches immediately due west of MT Rainier.

With all the signs coming to pass that Christ instructed us to watch for, few Christians comprehend just how close the end is. Earthquakes, extreme weather, the heat of the sun, pandemics, persecution of Jews and Christians, wars and rumor of war, lawlessness, globalism, drunkenness, sexual perversion, and corruption. Like the days of Noah, the American culture is soaked with entertainment, buying, and selling, marrying, and given in marriage—the masses are acting like zombies heading nowhere with no concerns.

This message about MT Rainier got its start through a dream I had during the week of March 25th, 2012. In the dream, the Puget Sound area of the Northwest was the location of volcanic activity that included earthquakes, lava flow, forest fires, ash, and bellowing smoke, making great portions of the land bleak and desolate. Ash covered most of the land and trees, and there were numerous forest fires.

The area in the dream was ringed by mountains just as it is in the Puget Sound area—ringed by the Cascade and Olympic Mountain ranges—but some of these mountains were spewing lava and erupting with volcanic activity.

In April of 2012, the content of this message was put in book format for private distribution, thinking that word of mouth was the appropriate way to bring forth the message.

Then in May of 2014, I had another dream that was more specific and very detailed. This dream led to updating the original book and was assigned an ISBN making it available for retail distribution.

-1-

Mount Rainier Erupting and Spewing Lava

In my second dream I was looking south towards Seattle from afar, in some house near the Mt. Vernon area, at least that was my sense of location. The Seattle skyline with the space needle was vivid, and Mount Rainier towered in the background. In this scene, Mount Rainier began to bellow

Seattle skyline, Space Needle, and Mt Rainier in background

smoke (perhaps ash) from its western slope, and then suddenly the smoke or ash turned to molten lava spewing forth.

In the forefront of this scene (within the house), the TV and Internet suddenly stopped, then a second or two later these two mediums resumed broadcasting and operating as normal, then the dream ended.

Since the first dream back in March 2012, our ministry team has been praying for more time: More time to prepare and warn and praying that the Pacific Northwest portion of the Ring of Fire would not ignite all at once.

I believe God has answered our prayers, that not everything will go at once. However, the most prominent and beautiful mountain in this area will start an eruption as a very strong warning—indeed God is about to start shouting for his people to wake up.

With this coming eruption of Mount Rainier, life will momentarily freeze, communications will be lost, and this event will stun millions as the news media in TV, radio, and Internet become obsessed with the event. The devastation will be massive.

Indeed, many will believe at first that this is judgment; however, as the news cycles spin forward coming to their end, life for the rest of America and the world will go back to normal. However, the people in the Puget Sound region of the Northwest will have a very difficult time.

A Desensitized Culture – an Asleep Church

Most Americans will watch with no emotion, unconsciously looking on like watching another disaster movie.

In the end times, Jesus said the culture of the world (including America) would become like it was in the days of Noah. *"For as were the days of Noah, so will be the coming of the Son of Man. For as in those days before the flood they were eating and drinking, marrying and giving in marriage, until the day when Noah entered the ark, and they were unaware until the flood came and swept them all away, so will be the coming of the Son of Man"* (Matthew 24:37-39).

In the days of Noah, the world's culture had evolved into extreme perversion, demonic manifestations, violence, and lawlessness. All sensitivity to morality and conscience were drowned in filth, perversion, and violence, with the people not taking pause to Noah's warnings. Then the flood came as judgment.

Today's immoral culture is also becoming like that of Sodom, where oppression, revenge, and persecution falls upon anyone who disagrees with the egregious homosexual agenda. The people in Sodom took offense to Lot's pleadings to stop the attempted homosexual gang rape of his visitors.

Instead of stopping, the homosexual mob threatened to do worse to Lot for confronting their evil agenda. The people of Sodom had completely given themselves to evil and perversion, opposing any restraint.

The "prior to judgment" cultures in the past, as well as now give virtually no pause to warnings by the prophets, and in these last days few give heed to the birth pangs judgments now coming upon America and the world.

The coming eruption of Mount Rainier, like the 9/11 towers falling, will only momentarily rock the conscience of America and shake sleeping Christians momentarily, then most will resume their indulgent lifestyles and carnal-driven church programs.

Since the early 1970s, when a move of God came upon many and when David Wilkerson published *The Vision*, prophesies about the Northwest Puget Sound region being devastated by volcanic activity and earthquakes abounded.

For years scientists have also warned of faults and tectonic plate movement in this area being heightened to a potential catastrophic volcanic and earthquake event. The scientific community cannot predict a time frame, yet a major fault shift could happen at any time.

However, God created and controls all the earth's nature and all its activities; all its mysteries and potential disasters are in God's providence, not by unpredictable happenstance as if produced by mother nature or some mother-earth goddess.

Past Prophesies

Again, in the 1970s, at a time when the Holy Spirit moved across the nation, many prophesies warned of devastating earthquakes in the Northwest and Puget Sound region.

Many thought that the MT St. Helens' eruption was the fulfillment of those prophesies. When it blew on May 18, 1980, it was the deadliest to date and most economically destructive volcanic eruption in the history of the United States. The explosion spewed ash across eleven states, killed 57 people and caused over a billion dollars in property damage.

Mount St. Helens' Eruption

The Pacific Northwest Ring of Fire is a small part of the larger Pacific Ring of Fire. These terms are used by scientists to explain the increasing earthquake and volcanic activity that is frequently shown in the news.

The scientific community continually warns of a coming cataclysmic seismic event to the Pacific Northwest but has no way of predicting when.

Pacific Ring of Fire Map

Birth Pangs of the Coming Kingdom

However, God knows when these events will occur and soon, He will allow events to happen in the Pacific Northwest and the Puget Sound region. Chile, Bolivia, Mexico, Japan, New Zealand, and the Philippines all have had recent birth-pang earthquake events. And now God will be raising his voice once again to warn Christians in this nation by allowing the Pacific Northwest Ring of Fire to be ignited.

Despite all the warnings, both prophetic and scientific, since the 70s, God's people are still complacent. Most leaders and pastors mislead Christians to believe God is silent on these kinds of matters. However, those who mislead will soon be rebuked, just as God warned the complacent men through Zephaniah in his day: *"At that time I will search Jerusalem with lamps, and I will punish the men who are complacent, those who say in their hearts, 'The Lord will not do good, nor will he do ill'"* (Zephaniah 12:1).

God is about to Raise his Voice

This warning is to awaken Christians and help them see that this looming disaster is about to take place as part of the birth pangs that Christ predicted, pointing to the final days of this age. Afflictions, distress, pandemics, perplexities of the nations and the upheaval of nature are meant to awaken God's people from complacency and to remind us that Christ's return is looming. God is raising his voice to warn that great trouble is about to come upon the whole world, including Christians.

This message is not a scare-tactic to drum up support for our work in ministry. It is not a false alarm to make people panic and do irrational things out of fear and confusion. It is not given to cause people to follow this ministry or myself as if it were the new thing in the so-called prophetic movement.

I do not take lightly the task of warning others concerning looming destruction. False alarmists and false prophets abound in these last days, just as Christ warned. It is up to you to seek confirmation from the Lord so that you may become convinced and act—I will not defend this warning or try to convince you to believe it or act in any way about it. You must hear from the Lord for yourself, for he said, *"My sheep hear my voice."*

We are mere bondservants of Christ who do his bidding and help those who follow Christ grow into the fullness of life in Christ. To help others become prepared and able to stand before him in his appearance.

This message is a warning of a coming event that many already believe will happen at some time, sooner or later. The timing of this coming event is under the sovereign control of the God of Abraham, Isaac and Jacob and the Father of our Lord and Savior Jesus Christ—the God of all creation who still warns through his prophets.

Let those who have an ear, hear what the Spirit is saying to the churches, to become prepared calmly and prayerfully as the voice of Christ instructs.

The key to safely navigate this coming event, as with the entire end of the age turmoil, is to know the true Christ, hear his voice, and obey. We must embrace all his words, know Scripture, and develop a Christ-like character through his discipline that produces obedience. (See Hebrews 12:7-11.)

Living Within MT Rainier's Lahar Danger Zones?
May 2018 update

Though this warning was published in 2014, we did nothing to promote this prophetic message. With the May 2018 volcanic activity starting up on the Big Island of Hawaii, the Lord prompted me to send this message to those who will be most affected by MT Rainier's eruption.

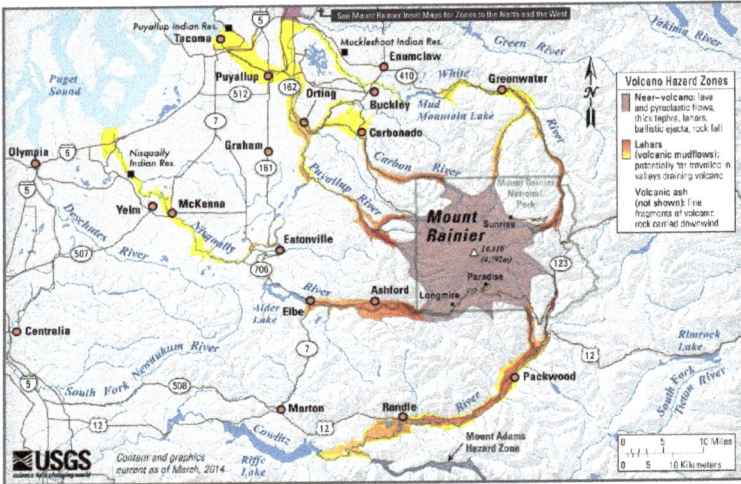

Mount Rainier Lahar Danger Zone Map

The populations surrounding the greater Puget Sound region will suffer from ash fallout, earthquakes and tremors, fires, deadly fumes, as well as terrible living conditions in a post volcanic disaster environment.

This prophetic warning is primarily meant for the masses of people who live, work, or own businesses within MT Rainier's volcanic mudflow paths. These people are the most at risk of dying almost instantly.

We are conveying this prophetic warning for those living in the projected lahar danger zones, specifically for Christian leadership to act and warn those in their care. In addition, we will attempt to share this warning with major Christian media ministries—to get the message out further.

Scientists, seismologists, and volcanologists studying MT Rainier's history have set up early warning systems for people living in MT Rainier's likely volcanic mudflow paths.

Despite the government warning systems now in place, scientists estimate that over 20,000 people will suffer loss of life. Rainier poses extreme risk to life and property, as many communities are situated atop older lahar deposits. View History Channel's video on YouTube entitled: *Mount Rainier Volcano is a Ticking Time Bomb – 2015 Documentary*. Viewing this 44-minute video will help one understand and hopefully take to heart Mt. Rainer's deadly destructive force.

Why the prophetic warning for Christians living in these lahar destruction zones? The lahar warning system reacts and warns after the event begins, after the mudflows start. This warning system gives just minutes to evacuate to higher ground.

For example, people living in the town of Orting will have maybe 40 minutes to rush to higher safe ground. The 30 ft wall of volcanic mudflow travels at 40 miles per hour. Highways will be jammed, people running to safety will be overtaken by ash and pumice mixed into hot concrete-like mud, carrying all manners of debris.

Therefore, scientists calculate that up to 20,000 or more people will lose their life in this wall of volcanic mud that will not stop until it hits Puget Sound.

God's Warning System

Scientists know Rainier is overdue to erupt, but they do not know when. However, God does know, and he warns through his prophets. When MT Rainier begins to increase earthquake activity (swarms of small earthquakes and larger tremors) and others initial indicators, then know that it is time to make way to high ground by relocating in advance or finding a place to stay temporarily.

Many will say it won't happen; however, the Lord is saying it will happen this time. If people wait until Rainier blows, it will be too late for many to run or drive to safety. Staying in shelter will not save anyone caught in the path of a lahar mudflow tsunami.

God does still warn through his servants, and He expects those in leadership to hear from God for themselves by confirming with the Lord concerning prophesy. If confirmed, then they are held accountable to be led by the Holy Spirit in helping others in their care, to be ready.

This prophesy was given to pastors and elders who minister and live in MT Rainier lahar danger zones—that they might warn and work with others—to pray, seek God's direction and become ready to flee to safety before MT Rainier erupts.

-3-
God is Raising His Voice
Is Anyone Listening?

God's people are aloof to the signs of Christ's soon return, only a few are awake. Most are too busy playing church: they are drunk on entertaining worship; they are numbed by empty manifestations from counterfeiting spirits; and they are burdened with the cares of this life. God's people are in love with this present age and are ignoring God's voice.

Most Christians: Evangelical, Charismatics, and Pentecostals alike—are lukewarm and unprepared for what is about to happen. Their ears are full of the voices of false alarmists and false prophets who are speaking forth errant warnings on behave of God when God has not spoken.

Many promote lies of false peace and never-ending prosperity, or quick-fix gimmicks laced with false doctrine. The good news of the coming kingdom and how to prepare for the terrible trouble leading to the rapture is now taboo; ignored, attacked, or dismissed as lies.

A remnant of sold-out disciples, preachers, and teachers cry out warnings, however their voices are muffled, gagged, cancelled, or completely squelched.

Where is the prophetic voice speaking from the pulpits, to cause God's people to awaken? Instead, most turn a deaf ear to the truth in Scripture. With closed hearts, they cannot hear the Holy Spirit's voice in the written Word and see the end-of-this-age predictions of Christ coming to pass.

And even as the signs of the end of this age are screaming *wake up.* God's people prefer to hear myths and lies to maintain gross denial. So now, God is about to raise his voice!

Fire and Brimstone Spewing

Jesus said of this hour, *"See that no one leads you astray. For many will come in my name, saying, 'I am the Christ,' and they will lead many astray. And you will hear of wars and rumors of wars. See that you are not alarmed, for this must take place, but the end is not yet. For nation will rise against nation, and kingdom against kingdom, and there will be famines and earthquakes in various places. All these are but the beginning of the birth pains"* (Matthew 24:4-8).

God in his faithfulness is about to wake up more of his people by raising his voice to another level, using earthshaking signs. The earth will soon recoil again and again to awaken a sleeping church to help gather his lost sheep in a rebellious world. God will allow violent earthquakes and volcanic activity that is beyond any modern historical precedence.

All the recent devastating earthquakes in various places will seem minor compared to this next round of shaking. In some areas of the world, the air, land, and sea will shake and spew volcanic eruptions, causing millions to take pause with a sense of doom.

The Spirit of God will bestow a weird surreal spiritual aura upon those directly affected and upon millions gazing at the media coverage—which will cause many to be unnerved. Vapor, smoke, and ash will be as the solemn voice of God, collaborating with the witness of the Spirit of God moving upon the wayward and ordinary un-churched person.

Northwest Ring of Fire Ignited

The specifics given to me over a period of one week back in March 2012, when I first received this warning from the Lord, pointed to extreme volcanic and earthquake activity in the Pacific Northwest, in the Puget Sound region.

Scientists for years have been convinced that the potential for earthquake and volcanic activity in this area of North America is highly likely. However, in their finite secular understanding they cannot predict when "mother nature" will do her thing.

They ignore God and his Word, relegating the God of creation to a myth. Science, in every aspect, has elevated man's knowledge to a position of all knowing, where the earth is worshipped. Indeed, science leads most to worship God's creation instead of the Creator.

The Pacific Northwest Ring of Fire consists of active faults and volcanic mountains and is a small part of the Pacific Ring of Fire that lies within nations, continents, and islands all around the Pacific Ocean.

In the Pacific Northwest area of the United States, America's portion

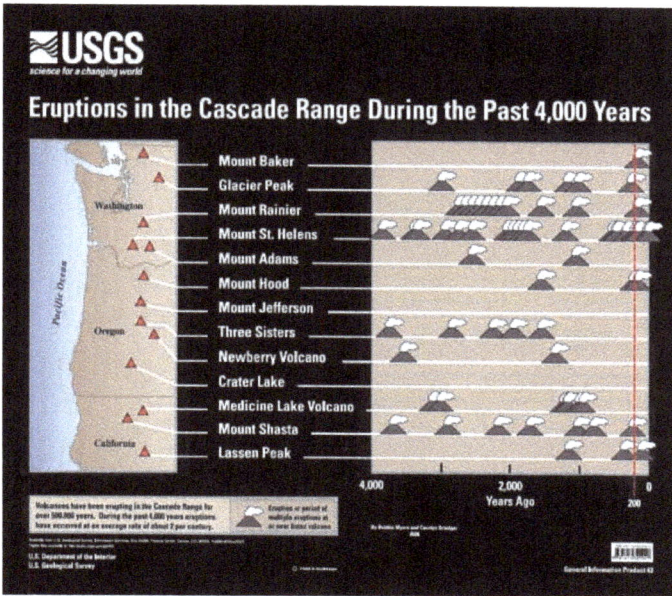

consists of the seven active or potentially active volcanoes. The most northern volcanos are Mt. Baker and Glacier Peak then going south comes Mt. Rainier, then Mt. Saint Helens and Mt. Adams, which are all in the state of Washington, followed by Mt. Hood in Oregon and finally Mt. Shasta in Northern California.

The Olympic Mountains are located between Puget Sound and the Pacific Ocean. This mountain range is not volcanic; however, due to the fault activity associated with this mountain range, scientists are expecting a quake they call the "Big One" to hit this area at any time.

Now God is going to set in motion his creation, the earth, to warn of who He is and point again to His sovereignty. God is about to demonstrate his control, cause shock and awe, resulting in fear, panic, and economic disarray for the people of the Northwest that will ripple out to the nation and around the world.

In my first dream, I saw lava flowing from various places in the Cascade mountain range and earthquakes in the Olympic Mountains—all around the Puget Sound area. Smoke, ash, and earthquakes accompanied the volcanic activity. There was also chaos caused by forest fires, mudflows, and evacuations. (In my follow-up dream in 2014, as stated in the introduction, Mount Rainier was the first to start this activity.)

I am not sure exactly when this will begin; however, it will be soon enough—time is running out to prepare. For Christians and churches impacted, the word given to me is prayer, repentance, and become ready.

(Delays concerning true prophetic warnings is God's mercy to allow His people to wake up and prepare.)

Christians are to stop blaming the lost, the homosexual agenda, abortions and all the other secular wickedness for these judgments—it is God's people playing church, living in secret sin, embracing carnal-driven church growth programs and being in love with this world that has ignited God's anger. The Holy Spirit is saying, "Repent, repent."

Those who receive this message must seek the Lord for repentance. May it not be shallow, but truly a heartfelt brokenness with deep life changing contriteness, for the kingdom of God is at hand, and its physical coming is soon!

Many Christians are lukewarm and at great risk of being spewed out of Christ's mouth—and many will be locked out of the coming marriage feast because they did not take enough oil to trim their lamps to see in the coming dark hour—as the midnight darkness becomes devoid of any light.

The Truth of God Ignored

Multitudes are headed for the valley of decision during the coming Great Tribulation. Millions upon millions of Christians will also be thrown into this terrible time—a time that will purify a polluted and lukewarm church.

Contrary to the popular false doctrine of a pre-tribulation rapture, Christ will rescue the true and purified saint at the *end* of the Great Tribulation period, just before God's wrath is poured out upon the whole world. (Jesus said of the Great Tribulation; *"And if the Lord had not cut short the days, no human being would be saved. But for the sake of the elect, whom he chose, he shortened the days"* (Mark 13:20).

Unfortunately, few Christians understand that they are expected to endure this coming time of trouble and to work in the final harvest of souls, as the age of the Gentiles comes to its close. Theologians, Christian authors, and pastors in pulpits everywhere have ignored, opposed, and even vilified those who preach this vital truth about the end of this age.

-4-
"Ungifted" Prophetic Tongues
Prophesies of Destruction from the Wayward

Because the voice of God has been virtually shut down within the church, God's Spirit is about to come upon the wayward, the lost, and the unchurched in the form of prophesy.

Ordinary people witnessing this next round of birth pangs will prophesy warnings of destruction and the coming of Christ and the wrath of God.

Many who hear this wave of God's prophetic voice coming from people who never had such experiences will be stunned at the ways God will speak—strange words, dreams, and visions.

Some will respond by seeking Christ, while many will shake it all off and try to get back to normal living, even as more and more reports of earthquake damage and volcanic eruptions flood the media air waves and Internet.

For those prophesying, only a small percentage will take heed themselves. However, many lost sinners and backslidden and lukewarm Christians will wake up and begin to call upon Christ. They will seek the truth and ask for help to become ready.

Instead of taking heed during these birth pang warnings and preparing to endure the coming tough times—a multitude of blinded Christians will become more excited about being raptured at any minute.

Blinded by false doctrines and false shepherds, many will continue to ignore the truth and become more complacent, lazy, and arrogant.

In some cases, celebrations of Christ's soon return will evolve into *rapture parties* where many deceived believers will arrogantly invite people to these entertaining events and pressure the bewildered lost sinner to become saved before they find themselves *left behind*.

Unfortunately, these supposedly on-fire Evangelical-Charismatic-Pentecostal Christians are lukewarm. Where many in this condition will fall into the company of those Christ spoke of as being deceived, who will say to Christ: *"Lord, Lord, did we not prophesy in your name, and cast out demons in your name, and do many mighty works in your name?' And then will I declare to them, 'I never knew you; depart from me, you workers of lawlessness'"* (Matthew 7:22-23).

The True Messengers of Christ are Coming

Delivering the Midnight Cry Message!

God is not going to leave the sincere Christian asleep and spellbound by false doctrines and entertaining churchianity. Soon he will send out a call to wake up his people to say, come away from the false.

True messengers who are in waiting and many who are still in training will soon be released with the unction of the Holy Spirit. They will be heralding the good news of the coming kingdom, teaching how to get right with the true Christ.

They have enough extra oil to brighten their lamps and see clearly in the coming end-of-the-age midnight hour. These true messengers of Christ are those spoken of in the parable of the ten virgins (Matthew 25:1-13). They will appear from nowhere as servants of Christ (the Bridegroom) and proclaim, *"Behold, the bridegroom! Come out to meet him."*

Christians will awaken to the coming message brought forth by these true servants of Christ. Many will realize they do not have a Christlike nature formed within them—much like the five foolish maidens from the parable who did not take extra oil for their lamps.

Some, who wake up unprepared may find grace to work out a true relationship with Christ with just enough time to prepare. These will have to embrace the intense troubles of the Great Tribulation by faith in Christ and embrace extra suffering. However, most will panic and buy into the antichrist lies and embrace the coming New World Order. They will cling to government help to make their way in the coming terrible darkness and desperate times.

These unprepared and foolish Christians will panic due to lack of faith, lack of Christlike character, and ignorance of God's word. They will put their faith in the false church and the antichrist lies and find themselves locked out of the wedding feast and hear these horrific words by our Lord: *"Truly, I say to you, I do not know you."*

5

Buy from Christ, Gold Refined in Fire

America's prosperity is ebbing away under affliction after affliction while a lukewarm church looks on nonchalantly. Many are beginning to see their life savings and retirements disintegrate right before their eyes. Millions, both Christians and unbelievers have started to buy gold and other precious metals as a hedge against a looming collapse of the economy. When the current economic boom suddenly collapses, as another sign Christ warned of, even then few will take heed.

Christians are overconfident, arrogant, and haughty, pointing the finger, full of carnal spiritual power, and do not realize they will be required to endure a great portion of the Great Tribulation.

Just like the church of Laodicea, Christians in America and many other places around the world consider themselves prosperous and in need of nothing.

Most Christians are blind to the coming devastations and will soon feel the wrath of the devil, as he will be allowed to set up his new world order in the coming judgments and tribulations, as he ruthlessly makes war on the saints.

Gold, silver, and 401Ks or hiding out in the wilderness will not deliver you from the coming trouble. For those reading this warning—if you have an ear to hear—the only way to survive the coming catastrophes is to do just as Christ instructed the Christians attending the church in Laodicea:

"Buy from me gold refined by fire, so that you may be rich, and white garments so that you may clothe yourself and the shame of your nakedness may not be seen, and salve to anoint your eyes, so that you may see. Those whom I love, I reprove and discipline, so be zealous and repent. Behold, I stand at the door and knock. If anyone hears my voice and opens the door, I will come in to him and eat with him, and he with me. The one who conquers, I will grant him to sit with me on my throne, as I also conquered and sat down with my Father on his throne. He who has an ear, let him hear what the Spirit says to the churches" (Revelation 3:18-22).

If you hear what the Holy Spirit is saying to God's people, then repent and buy from Christ gold refined in the fires of his discipline.

Give Christ permission to chastise and reprove you. Allow him to expose your carnality, all ill-motives, pride of life, and arrogant self-righteous attitudes.

Allow Christ to show you how much you are in love with this present age and the trappings of this world. Many are in love with working for the church and being religious yet not allowing Christ to develop a true relationship with our heavenly Father. A multitude of believers are not instructed in the discipline of the Lord, that allows Christlike character formed within, replacing the old carnal character. (See Galatians 4:17-20.)

Time is running out for buying into God's way of being prepared. True faith in Christ and Christlike character refined by fire is the only hedge against the coming troubles. Embrace Christ's discipline and allow him to guide you, which will give you access to his protection and provision.

"But watch yourselves lest your hearts be weighed down with dissipation and drunkenness and cares of this life, and that day come upon you suddenly like a trap. For it will come upon all who dwell on the face of the whole earth. But stay awake at all times, praying that you may have strength to escape all these things that are going to take place, and to stand before the Son of Man" (Luke 21:34-36).

The word "strength" in the underlined section above means becoming *qualified* or *worthy* to escape all these things. Many Christians have misunderstood the grace of God and even outraged the Spirit of grace by maintaining their carnality as they go on sinning deliberately, under *false cheap-grace* teachings.

Becoming worthy of God's grace does not imply religious works and acts of goodness to be justified before God. We must learn to work out our own salvation in fear and trembling and become doers of the word, not just hearers.

Buying from Christ gold refined in fire means undertaking the trials and the discipline that purifies the heart, soul, and spirit. This is what makes one eligible or qualified for his favor and guidance in the dark days ahead.

Wake Up Now—Before the Midnight Cry

If you think this warning is not for you, then think twice. If you continue to take your ease, continue to follow false teachers who tickle the ear; if you then expect God to deliver you, yet reject this and other like-kind warnings—you will have no excuse. If you do not buy gold refined in the fire from Christ, it will have to come from suffering extra in the fires of the coming judgments and the terrors of the Great Tribulation.

The Christians of the church of Philadelphia suffered and yet kept Christ's word and did not deny his name—and because they kept his word of patience endurance, Christ promised, *"I will keep you from the hour of trial coming upon the whole world"* (Revelation 3:10).

Being kept by Christ in the coming tribulation and trials does not mean the rapture, but rather being miraculously protected, guided, provided for, and delivered. There will be suffering for all. Those who buy now from Christ, gold refined in fire willingly, will certainly suffer less than those who played church and allowed themselves to stay carnal, defiled, and in love with this age.

If you take the wide gate and easy path now, at least this truthful warning will remind you later why you did not escape the coming troubles. This warning and others like it will help you understand what is happening to you.

You will know why you and your family are suffering as believers, while Christ himself is more protective of those who took heed before the troubles came.

These warnings may keep you from buying into the antichrist lies, like the five foolish virgins who went out to the dealers to buy extra oil. When they returned, the door to wedding and eternity was shut—they were locked out.

False Doctrines and False Alarmists Deceiving Many

Even as the birth pangs and signs of Christ's coming increase, becoming obvious, as recorded in Scripture—few are taking heed. False prophets, false alarmists, and false teachings inspired by Satan have lulled most Christians to sleep. These false alarmists are like the boy who repeatedly cried "wolf" when none was nearby. This has caused many teachers and pastors to refrain from sounding any warning that the end-of-the-age is close at hand.

Now, when true warnings come, few will take heed and seek the Lord for confirmation and direction. You must test everything, even what I am writing and hear from God for yourself and then act accordingly.

Multitudes of deceived believers have bought into the pre-tribulation rapture myth made popular by such authors as Hal Lindsey, who wrote *Late Great Planet Earth* and Tim LaHaye and Jerry Jenkins, authors of the *Left Behind* series of books and movies. Believing in these false teachings put believers at great risk of being unprepared to meet Christ.

Those who believe these contradictions to Christ's own teachings on this matter truly fall into the "foolish virgin" category. The coming persecution prior to the Great Tribulation will force the insincere and the false believer to either fall away or get it right. For the true believer, their faith will develop into an undivided devotion to Christ, becoming pure in heart and prepared.

There are many who know of Christ but are not known by him. They have no fear of God or desire to become sanctified and transformed to have Christ's nature built within.

They are taking it easy, arrogantly prancing through life and believing they are sincerely following Christ. They are following the name of Christ but not allowing Christ to discipline and transform them—learning to die to their old carnal nature.

Unless Christ is allowed to truly change the inner person, to be truly known by Christ and abide in Him—Jesus warned that he would say to those in such a deceived spiritual condition, *"Truly I say to you, I do not know you."*

Christians have heard warnings over and over—yet life goes on. Because the bridegroom (the returning Christ) is delayed, most believers are slumbering, and many are "out cold"—sound asleep. Even now, as the signs of his coming scream GET READY, few are awake or prepared for his return. Jesus said, *"So also, when you see these things taking place, you know that he is near, at the very gates"* (Mark 13:29).

6

Three Kinds of Foolish Christians

At this moment in time there are basically three camps of foolish Christians: Those who ignore the signs and avoid watching, believing Christ's appearance will not be in their lifetime; those who anticipate their rescue before any trouble or suffering comes; and those who believe Christianity will convert the world and usher in the millennial rule of Christ.

In all cases, these Christians know about Christ, they follow their pastor or favorite teacher, and attend church, but they do not intimately know Christ or obey his voice. They are asleep and unprepared, being easily led astray.

At the end of the parable of the ten virgins, Christ warns, *"Watch therefore, for you know neither the day nor the hour"* (Matthew 25:13). Christ expects Christians to be aware of the times, to know the season of his return, and to be ready to endure the difficult dark days leading to that moment.

No one knows the day or hour of his coming, but Christ expects His disciples to know the season by watching, praying consistently, living in His holy presence, and being ready spiritually and physically for the coming difficult times. Like the wise virgins, the sincere Christian will have a genuine relationship with Christ that consists of true faith and obedience that springs from Christlike character.

The foolish maidens in our parable did not have the qualities of a true disciple. During the extreme darkness, and at the sound of the midnight cry, they realized they did not have extra oil to trim their lamps. They asked the wise maidens to share their extra oil, but the wise said no. A true disciple of Christ cannot share their Christlike character or impart faith to others.

The wise were ready, and the foolish were unprepared. The wise truly knew Christ. The foolish knew of Christ religiously and were forced to look elsewhere for extra oil. In the end, they were locked out of eternity.

Complacency and Love of this World

The power of the world: politics, buying and selling, marrying, raising a family, making a living, pursuing the American dream of home ownership, owning cars, having a comfortable lifestyle—has put multitudes of Christians at ease. Most of these endeavors are legitimate, but they have become idols of the heart, directly contradicting Christ's words: *"Do not lay up for yourselves treasures on earth, where moth and rust consume and where thieves break in and steal, but lay up for yourselves treasures in heaven, where neither moth nor rust consumes and where thieves do not break in and steal. For where your treasure is, there will your heart be also"* (Matthew 6:19-21).

The hearts of many Christians are in love with this world and complacent about Christ, the things of God, and the signs of his soon return. This condition puts them at great risk.

Jesus warned that, as in the days of Noah, the coming of the Son of Man would be in the same manner: *"For as in those days before the flood they were eating and drinking, marrying and giving in marriage, until the day when Noah entered the ark, and they did not know until the flood came and swept them all away, so will be the coming of the Son of man. ...Watch therefore, for you do not know on what day your Lord is coming"* (Matthew 24:38-42). This is the attitude of many believers today. They are having a good time, seeking prosperity, and enjoying life to the fullest—by integrating a compromised gospel into a worldly successful and prosperous lifestyle.

As the birth pangs increase, this type of believer will continue to flex their political muscle trying to preserve freedom, prosperity, and cultural morality. They show more interest in restoring Hollywood's morals and making Disneyland "pure again" than in becoming pure in Christ and avoiding the love of this world.

Christians push for sermons and church services that hold their attention with high entertainment value. Leaders are hired based on a flamboyant personality and the ability to teach how to live joyfully, making life on earth more pleasant.

These birth pangs are God speaking to his people— "Wake up now for the time is short!" Nevertheless, most Christians act like drunken sailors oblivious to the next day's hangover, unwilling to accept that the end is near. The coming Great Tribulation will be the final *wake-up call* and in which a multitude of lukewarm and backslidden Christians and masses of lost unbelievers will come to Christ in true salvation—before the rapture. The persecution leading into this terrible time will be used as a *vetting process* by God, causing the false believer to fall away.

Just Like it was in the Days of Sodom

All the signs of worldwide instability are in place as predicted in Scripture. One abhorrent sign that is a clear indication of the end being at the very gates is the sodomite control and influence in all levels of society — culturally, politically, legislatively, and judicially.

The homosexuals in Sodom seized control of the cities. Lot had no political, civil, or ethical rights to protect himself or his angelic guests. When Lot confronted their demands to sodomize his guests, this gang of homosexuals rebuffed and threatened Lot saying: *"'Stand back!' And they said, 'This fellow came to sojourn, and he would play the judge! Now we will deal worse with you than with them'"* (Genesis 19:9).

Now, in our society, those who speak out against the sodomite immorality sweeping the country are threatened just as Lot was threatened. These and other signs described by Christ and the apostles are coming to a crescendo — yet God's people are still sound asleep!

Unparalleled Earthquakes and Eruptions

The birth pangs of the coming kingdom are about to rise to a new level, taking the form of earthquakes and volcanic eruptions that will hurl smoke, ash, destruction, and brimstone (lava and sulfur) that will force many to take heed.

When this next level of warning comes to pass hopefully you will remember this prediction. Then my hope is, you will take to heart the rest of this warning, embrace correction, and submit to Christ's sanctifying disciplines.

Do not think that America is going to be saved while the rest of the world falls under the antichrist's rule? America is headed for judgment and will succumb to the coming New World Order rule, as the rest of the world falls in line.

7

The Fracturing of Christianity

The Great Falling Away of the Lukewarm and False

As the birth pangs of the coming kingdom increase, more Christians will wake up to the truth. God will open the eyes of the deceived good-hearted Christian. This awakening will result in schisms, divisions, and confusion. Fellowships and denominations throughout the so-called body of Christ will soon experience upheaval and an exodus of attendees.

With the increased birth pang judgments and increasing persecution, God's Spirit will work in concert with the true messengers of Christ and ignite the beginning of the last day's separation between the false and the true Christian.

Many lukewarm Christians will be shaken awake as God begins to raise his voice through these coming cataclysmic events. Jesus warned of this great fracturing within Christianity at the end of this age in Matthew 24:10-11: *"And then many will fall away and betray one another and hate one another. And many false prophets will arise and lead many astray."*

Just as the invisible faults along the Pacific Ring of Fire begin to fracture, God is about to fracture all of Christianity and begin to draw the true body of Christ away from the grossly deceived Christian and the false leader.

The true saint will begin to take to heart what Scripture states in the book of Hebrews concerning God shaking the earth and the heavens once more.

"See that you do not refuse him who is speaking. For if they did not escape when they refused him who warned them on earth, much less will we escape if we reject him who warns from heaven. At that time his voice shook the earth, but now he has promised, 'Yet once more I will shake not only the earth but also the heavens.' This phrase, "Yet once more," indicates the removal of things that are shaken—that is, things that have been made—in order that the things that cannot be shaken may remain. Therefore let us be grateful for receiving a kingdom that cannot be shaken, and thus let us offer to God acceptable worship, with reverence and awe, for our God is a consuming fire" (Hebrews 12:25-29).

This coming final awakening will become a valley of decision for many Christians. Many will be forced to decide between the truth concerning Christ's return and the falsehoods taught by leaders who have daubed the walls with whitewash, saying, "All is well for the Christian."

Christians will have to decide whether to believe what Scripture says about enduring to the end or continue to believe the false who preach never-ending prosperity, a protected America, and the rapture before the Great Tribulation.

Woe to the Whitewashing False Leader
The false shepherds will decry and vilify this warning

False shepherds and false national leaders have made a nice living off gullible and naïve Christians. These false leaders have prophesied from a greedy heart and their own spirit, telling God's people all is well. (See 2 Peter 2:1-3.)

This coming round of birth pangs is God raising his voice against the false leaders of today. Just like the false prophets condemned by God through Ezekiel: *"Your prophets have been like jackals among the ruins, O Israel. You have not gone up into the breaches, or built up a wall for the house of Israel, that it might stand in battle in the day of the Lord"* (Ezekiel 13:4-5).

With false doctrines, lying divinations, and false visions, whitewashing leaders of today lead God's people astray. They pronounce no end to peace and prosperity on earth. God's people are not prepared for battle on the day that God acts.

Therefore, God will allow a deluge of birth pang storms to crush the whitewashed wall of lies that have blinded and lulled His people to sleep.

Many false leaders will not go away without a fight, even as this next round of shaking on earth and in the heavens begins. With venom and fierce hate-filled bitterness, they will denounce this and other warnings as false, divisive, and negative.

In the name of protecting the sheep from such negativism many false leaders and false shepherds will network together and launch a campaign of lies, misrepresentation, and slander to vilify the true messengers of Christ and the Christian worker who speaks forth the truth.

In the coming days, the true saint must prepare for fierce opposition from false believers who will attack in outright hatefulness and bitter criticism. Brace for spiritual attacks that will come through the carnal prayers of those opposing this truth as they pray against those who speak forth the truth.

The false and carnal Christian who prays wrongly is practicing a form of sorcery. This is a very potent and insidious work of the flesh and one of the devil's most powerful weapons. Christians who do not pray according to

God's will in these coming days will be at risk of judgment for opposing God's true servants on the day that He acts.

Unity between Catholic and Protestants
New World Order Ecumenism and the Last Days Harlot Church

Another insidious work of Satan in these dark days is the current push for unity between all Christian denominations and the Catholic Church of Rome.

Popular but errant leaders such as Rick Warren, Kenneth Copeland, Franklin Graham, and many others are influencing Protestant Christians to embrace unity of fellowship and doctrinal acceptance with the Roman Catholic Church.

Contemplative, purpose driven, dominion, ecumenical theology, and other false doctrines over the last forty years slowly formed this unity movement that is now growing quickly.

David Wilkerson, in publishing a vision he received from the Lord in 1973, concerning end-time events, saw a super world church arise with great political influence, wielding oppressive powers.

Wilkerson saw great persecution coming against the true Christian preaching Christ's truth about the end of this age. The primary thrust to squelch the truth of Christ's return will come at the hands of this super church.

> Here is an excerpt from David Wilkerson's book, The Vision: "This super world church will be spiritual in name only, freely using the name of Jesus Christ, but will, in fact, be antichrist and political in many of its activities… I see an army of career people invading the most influential posts in this super church organization. Many of them will be ungodly, antichrist people, obsessed with the concept that this super church must become a political power, strong enough to put pressure on all those who oppose its actions. While those in the highest posts of leadership will be speaking about miracles, love, and reconciliation, hirelings who work under them will be harassing and persecuting those religious organizations opposed to their leadership." (*The Vision*, New York: Pyramid Communications, 1974 p.76-77)

The Apostle John saw a similar vision of an end-time great false church, which was depicted as a harlot having great influence upon multitudes of peoples, nations, and rulers.

A Depiction of John's vision of the Great Harlot

Many astute and sound theologians interpret this false super-ecumenical church as the false church described in Revelation starting in chapter 17, depicted as a harlot that sits upon many waters and works in concert with the beast and the antichrist in the soon to come New World Order: *"Then one of the seven angels who had the seven bowls came and said to me, 'Come, I will show you the judgment of the great harlot who is seated upon many waters, with whom the kings of the earth have committed fornication, and with the wine of whose fornication the dwellers on earth have become drunk.' And he carried me away in the Spirit into a wilderness, and I saw a woman sitting on a scarlet beast which was full of blasphemous names, and it had seven heads and ten horns. The woman was arrayed in purple and scarlet, and bedecked with gold and jewels and pearls, holding in her hand a golden cup full of abominations and the impurities of her fornication; and on her forehead was written a name of mystery: 'Babylon the great, mother of harlots and of earth's abominations.' And I saw the woman, drunk with the blood of the saints and the blood of the martyrs of Jesus. When I saw her I marveled greatly But the angel said to me, 'Why marvel? I will tell you the mystery of the woman, and of the beast with seven heads and ten horns that carries her'"* (Revelation 17:1-7 RSV).

Come Away from the False and Love Not the World

Reading on in Revelation 18, John hears in his vision a powerful angel calling out in a mighty voice. The angel is speaking of the coming destruction of the end-of-the-age super false church and its corrupt system of religion, politics, and economics that is soaked in immorality, greed, and luxurious living.

John also heard another voice from heaven saying, *"Come out of her, my people, lest you take part in her sins, lest you share in her plagues; for her sins are heaped high as heaven, and God has remembered her iniquities." (Revelation 18:4-5).*

Many of God's people are restricted from the fullness of Christ and His abundant life (fullness of life with Father God) because of carnal and worldly affections, in addition to the defilements that impinge upon their spirit affecting their spiritual life with God.

The false Christianity that they embrace keeps them defiled and in love with this world. The false super world church that is forming will become very powerful in galvanizing the lukewarm Christian into a *destiny of doom*.

Many try to serve God and money together, trying to maintain a prosperous worldly lifestyle. Christians carrying defilements from their former life will continue to be emotionally involved and spiritually enthralled with idolatrous living. Many now live in secret sins, while many flaunt a perverted lifestyle.

Also, many are held spell bound as they gaze upon the world's perverted cultures and wayward lifestyles, subtly titillated in fantasy and falling into secret sin, they search for Christian fellowship that accommodates the ways of the world.

Many have lost their faith since they repeatedly reject conscience. We continue to see on a nationwide scale scandals concerning pastors and Christian leaders falling from grace. Most fall victim to sin because of the false doctrine they embrace.

Now is the time to leave idolatry and sensuous living behind. Flee false Christianity and run to the true Christ, giving him permission to expose and cleanse all defilements, and be willing to leave the lukewarm and apostate churches. Seek out fellowship with likeminded believers and take no part in the unfruitful works of darkness.

The Apostle Paul instructed the Christians at Corinth using the following exhortation, *"Since we have these promises, beloved, let us cleanse ourselves from every defilement of body and spirit, bringing holiness to completion in the fear of God"* (2 Corinthians 7:1).

Christians today do not understand the importance of being cleansed from past impurities, or for that matter, few receive instruction on how to work out their salvation and grow up into Christ, learning to walk in true holiness.

Many cover up the old nature and their past uncleansed defilements and thus suffer from imbedded bitter jealousy and selfish motives—they learn to pretend and walk in self-righteous and carnal holiness.

God's people point their finger at the lost and the wicked yet look the other way concerning their own wickedness and secret sins. That is why so many are being overwhelmed by the flood of filth now spewing forth from the American culture turned sodomite.

America has lost its moral compass and is falling headlong towards fulfilling the evils predicted in Revelation, the Babylonian culture and the last day harlot church, its politics, and a perverted culture.

It is time to give up on America and stop fighting to preserve or restore its moral foundations. You will just get a sound thrashing. The moral majority and Christian influence have faded. What remains now is a whimpering moral minority, with evangelical Christians across America having less and less influence politically.

It was Dr. James Dobson, during his retirement speech on April 12, 2009, that supports this point when he stated, "We are awash in evil, and the battle is still to be waged. We are right now in the most discouraging period of that long conflict. Humanly speaking, we can say we have lost all those battles."

Since then, many have continued to wage a moral war and continue to lose battle after battle as the tide of filth continues. Unfortunately, few understand because they are stuck in denial to the fact that America has crossed the line.

A Kingdom that Cannot be Shaken

Dear saint, in all that is about to happen, know that God has set aside for us a kingdom that cannot be shaken, a spiritual realm on earth that is safe, which affects our physical world. This kingdom is for us to abide in now, as we await the coming of Christ and the physical manifestation of the Kingdom of God.

Until Christ appears, it will become terribly gloomy and seemingly hopeless upon earth in the coming days. As the birth pangs of the coming kingdom increase, and then as the Great Tribulation begins, false prophets with false signs will lead the unprepared Christian astray. There may be short lived moral corrections but those seemly glimmer of hope will add to the deception and keep the unprepared Christian asleep.

The coming deception will be so powerful; the elect of God will take pause and be tempted to give up and give in to the antichrist lies.

Do not give in to these lies but become determined and prepared to endure to the end. *"The one who endures to the end will be saved. And this gospel of the kingdom will be proclaimed throughout the whole world as a testimony to all the nations, and then the end will come"* (Matthew 24:13-14).

The coming fracturing within Christianity (the true Christian coming out from among the false) will once again distinguish the true Christian from the false and the true servant of God from the one who does not serve him.

The coming persecution by false Christians and the world, as well as evil perpetrated by the devil and his antichrist, during the coming Great Tribulation, is not God's wrath.

The Rapture is Part of God's Plan

The true saint and the true body of Christ are not destined for the wrath of God. Yes, there will be a rapture where the angels will be sent to gather true Christians and take them up into the air to be in the presence of Christ.

However, it will happen just before the wrath of God falls upon the earth as the Great Tribulation is cut short. *"But in those days, after that tribulation, … And then they will see the Son of Man coming in clouds with great power and glory. And then he will send out the angels and gather his elect from the four winds, from the ends of the earth to the ends of heaven"* (Mark 13:24-27). Thus, the Apostle Paul states that we await: *"For his Son from heaven, whom he raised from the dead, Jesus who delivers us from the wrath to come"* (1 Thessalonians 1:10).

-8-
Pray for More Time
The devil wants the end to come prematurely

Satan wants sincere but deceived Christians to stay in a weighted-down and deceived condition with the cares of this life blinding them to the hour. He wants them to keep living for self, not for Christ. If the devil can suddenly push the end to come before its time, then he will have destroyed many of God's people who were unprepared.

Satan tried to kill Jesus before his time. The devil had all the apostles arrested at the beginning of the church age, and he tried to murder Peter before his time.

However, God warned Joseph in a dream to flee danger, taking Mary and baby Jesus to Egypt. Divine intervention came for the apostles as an angel of the Lord opened prison doors and brought the apostles out, giving them instruction to stand before the people in the temple and preach the Gospel! (See Acts 5:17-21 and 12:1-17 concerning the Apostles and Peter.)

As for Herod's attempt to kill Peter to please the Jews, the church made earnest prayer for him. Thus, the very night that Herod was to bring Peter out to be executed, again, the angel of the Lord appeared. That angel slapped Peter on the side to wake him saying, *"Get up quickly,"* and he led Peter to safety, preempting another attempt by Satan to stop the Gospel from advancing.

This is the case now. The devil does not want the true Gospel of the coming Kingdom preached to the world before the end comes as Jesus prophesied, *"And this gospel of the kingdom will be preached throughout the whole world, as a testimony to all nations; and then the end will come"* (Matthew 24:14).

There is Much Work Ahead

These birth pangs taking place, coming upon the whole world in the form of perplexing troubles, great earthquakes, persecution, pandemics, and a soon to come global economic crisis is God warning us and slapping his people awake, saying, "Get ready quickly. There is much work to do."

You and I have work to do, if America falls completely in an instant, our work will not be accomplished. Satan wants the end to come early before God's people are awake and ready. The devil's plan is to preempt the last move of God and the final awakening with a premature economic collapse and destruction of America. We must pray earnestly for more time to get ready!

Find Likeminded Fellowship—Now!

Pastor, if you are not warning and teaching sound doctrine on how to prepare God's people God's way, then expect sincere believers to leave. They will be searching for like-minded fellowship.

For true believers in a false fellowship, do not try to correct leadership, they are most likely scoffing at the truth and all you will get is abuse.

Those preaching a pre-tribulation rapture before any real trouble, are deceived and are most likely a false shepherd. They are part of the problem and at best they are not reliable shepherds. Flee and seek Christ for direction.

If you cannot find a sound fellowship near you, then pray for direction in meeting other like-minded Christians and then pray about forming a home fellowship.

May the Lord's light shine upon you, guide and protect you and your loved ones in these coming dark days.

Contact Information

Mailing address:
MC Global Ministries
PO Box 857, Canon City, CO 81215

www.ingramcontent.com/pod-product-compliance
Lightning Source LLC
Chambersburg PA
CBHW042102060426
42446CB00046B/3470